N. T. WRIGHT
FOR EVERYONE
BIBLE STUDY GUIDES

JAMES

9 STUDIES FOR INDIVIDUALS AND GROUPS

N. T. WRIGHT

WITH PHYLLIS J. LE PEAU

IVP Connect

An imprint of InterVarsity Press
Downers Grove, Illinois

InterVarsity Press
P.O. Box 1400, Downers Grove, IL 60515-1426
World Wide Web: www.ivpress.com
E-mail: email@ivpress.com

This study guide is based on and includes excerpts adapted from The Early Christian Letters for
Everyone, © 2011 Nicholas Thomas Wright. All New Testament quotations, unless otherwise indicated,
are taken from The Kingdom New Testament published in the United States by HarperOne and from
The New Testament for Everyone published in England by SPCK; copyright © 2011 by Nicholas
Thomas Wright. Used by permission of SPCK, London. All rights reserved.

InterVarsity Press® is the book-publishing division of InterVarsity Christian Fellowship/USA®, a
movement of students and faculty active on campus at hundreds of universities, colleges and schools
of nursing in the United States of America, and a member movement of the International Fellowship of
Evangelical Students. For information about local and regional activities, write Public Relations Dept.,
InterVarsity Christian Fellowship/USA, 6400 Schroeder Rd., P.O. Box 7895, Madison, WI 53707-7895, or
visit the IVCF website at <www.intervarsity.org>.

Design: Cindy Kiple
Cover image: Karl Weatherly/Getty Images

ISBN 978-0-8308-2196-9

Printed in the United States of America ∞

 InterVarsity Press is committed to protecting the environment and to the responsible use of
natural resources. As a member of Green Press Initiative we use recycled paper whenever
possible. To learn more about the Green Press Initiative, visit <www.greenpressinitiative.org>.

P	20	19	18	17	16	15	14	13	12	11	10	9	8	7	6	5	4
Y	29	28	27	26	25	24	23	22	21	20	19	18	17	16	15		

CONTENTS

GETTING THE MOST
OUT OF JAMES

We don't know for sure who James was. It was as common a name in the first century as it is today. But there is a strong chance that this letter was from the best-known James in the early church: James the brother of Jesus, the strong central leader in the Jerusalem church over the first thirty years of Christianity. Peter and Paul and the others went off around the world, but he stayed put in Jerusalem, praying and teaching and trusting that the God who had raised his beloved brother from the dead would complete what he had begun. This letter, then, would be part of that work, written to encourage Christians across the world—whom he saw as the new version of the "twelve dispersed tribes" of Israel—to face up to the challenge of faith.

One of the great themes of the letter is patience. Another theme in parallel with patience is wisdom. James is the most obvious representative in the New Testament of what in the ancient Israelite Scriptures (the Old Testament) we think of as "wisdom literature": the sifted, tested and collected wisdom of those who learned to trust God for everything and to discover how that trust would work out in every aspect of daily life. The followers of Jesus believed the Old Testament had all come rushing together with new meaning in the life, death and resurrection of their lord and master.

In this letter, James asks what will last, what is permanent. His answer is clear: God and his Word. This is urgently needed, because without it we look (metaphorically) at beautiful wild flowers which spring up out in the open country: here today and gone tomorrow, or even sooner if the sun is hot. We look at them and think they are what matters. We will see people becoming rich and famous, with fine houses, big cars and luxurious holidays. Today's celebrity culture tells its own story. A famous sports hero one day, out on the street the next; a flashy wedding one day, a messy divorce the next. We know these stories and yet we are seduced by the glitter of it all . . . by the beauty of the wild flowers which passes away.

Another of James's key themes is the dangerous power of the human tongue. This is all a piece of what he says about God's Word. His Word is not just conveying information; it actually does things, brings about a new and lasting state of affairs. So we see God's Word going to work even as we hear a warning about our human words going to work in a rather different direction.

Throughout the letter James talks about faith. Faith that works and praying in faith which surrounds all that we are and do as followers of Jesus. Everything that James says flows from the astonishing fact that his older brother, Jesus himself, had embodied new life and forgiveness. Jesus had hung at the place where new life and forgiveness came bursting through from God's world to ours. (For more on this letter also see my *The Early Christian Letters for Everyone* published by SPCK and Westminster John Knox, on which this guide is based. New Testament quotations in this guide are from my own translation, published as *The Kingdom New Testament* by HarperOne in the United States and published as *The New Testament for Everyone* by SPCK in England.)

As we learn from James through this guide (prepared with the help of Phyllis J. Le Peau, for which I am grateful), we seek to understand and obey "the royal law" of love and to get to know Jesus himself. And as that happens, so the patience and humility, the love and the prayer, the wisdom and the true speech on which he has been insisting will become part of our lives. These are the works which will demonstrate faith. Even as James was written to encourage Christians across the world to face up to the challenge of faith, may you be encouraged in the same way and grow as people of faith as you study this letter.

SUGGESTIONS FOR INDIVIDUAL STUDY

1. As you begin each study, pray that God will speak to you through his Word.

2. Read the introduction to the study and respond to the "Open" question that follows it. This is designed to help you get into the theme of the study.

3. Read and reread the Bible passage to be studied. Each study is designed to help you consider the meaning of the passage in its context. The commentary and questions in this guide are based on my own translation of each passage found in the companion volume to this guide in the For Everyone series on the New Testament (published by SPCK and Westminster John Knox).

4. Write your answers to the questions in the spaces provided or in a personal journal. Each study includes three types of questions: observation questions, which ask about the basic facts in the passage; interpretation questions, which delve into the meaning of the passage; and application questions, which help you discover the implications of the text for growing in Christ. Writing out your responses can bring clarity and deeper understanding of yourself and of God's Word.

5. Each session features selected comments from the For Everyone series. These notes provide further biblical and cultural background and contextual information. They are designed not to answer the questions for you but to help you along as you study the Bible for yourself. For even more reflections on each passage, you may wish to have on hand a copy of the companion volume from the For Everyone series as you work through this study guide.

6. Use the guidelines in the "Pray" section to focus on God, thanking him for what you have learned and praying about the applications that have come to mind.

SUGGESTIONS FOR GROUP MEMBERS

1. Come to the study prepared. Follow the suggestions for individual study mentioned above. You will find that careful preparation will greatly enrich your time spent in group discussion.

2. Be willing to participate in the discussion. The leader of your group will not be lecturing. Instead, she or he will be asking the questions found in this guide and encouraging the members of the group to discuss what they have learned.

3. Stick to the topic being discussed. These studies focus on a particular passage of Scripture. Only rarely should you refer to other portions of the Bible or outside sources. This allows for everyone to participate on equal ground and for in-depth study.

4. Be sensitive to the other members of the group. Listen attentively when they describe what they have learned. You may be surprised by their insights! Each question assumes a variety of answers. Many questions do not have "right" answers, particularly questions that aim at meaning or application. Instead the questions push us to explore the passage more thoroughly.

   When possible, link what you say to the comments of others. Also, be affirming whenever you can. This will encourage some of the more hesitant members of the group to participate.

5. Be careful not to dominate the discussion. We are sometimes so eager to express our thoughts that we leave too little opportunity for others to respond. By all means participate! But allow others to also.

6. Expect God to teach you through the passage being discussed and through the other members of the group. Pray that you will have an enjoyable and profitable time together, but also that as a result of the study you will find ways that you can take action individually and/ or as a group.

7. It will be helpful for groups to follow a few basic guidelines. These

guidelines, which you may wish to adapt to your situation, should be read at the beginning of the first session.

- Anything said in the group is considered confidential and will not be discussed outside the group unless specific permission is given to do so.

- We will provide time for each person present to talk if he or she feels comfortable doing so.

- We will talk about ourselves and our own situations, avoiding conversation about other people.

- We will listen attentively to each other.

- We will be very cautious about giving advice.

Additional suggestions for the group leader can be found at the back of the guide.

1

THE CHALLENGE OF FAITH

James 1:1-8

I used to think the waves had come from far away. Standing by the sea and watching the gray-green monsters roll in, it was easy to imagine that this wave, and then this one, and then the one after that, had made the journey from a distant land. Here they were, like the Magi, arriving at last to deposit their gifts.

But of course it isn't like that. Waves are what happen when wind and tide take hold of the waters that are there all the time and make them dance to their tune. Just yesterday I stood in the bright sunshine and watched them sparkling and splashing around a little harbor, making the boats dip and bob. A fine sight; the waves seem to have character and energy of their own. But they don't. They are the random products of other forces. The challenge in faith is not to be a wave.

OPEN

What is it like to tossed by waves, whether inside a boat or just in the water?

STUDY

1. *Read James 1:1-8.* Quite a challenge it was in James's time to be a Christian, as it is now and always has been. The moment you decide to follow Jesus is the moment that you expect the trials and tribulations to begin. It's a bit like opening the back door to set off on a walk and finding that the wind nearly pushes you back inside before you've even started. And James tells us we should celebrate such moments (v. 2)! We should learn to look at them with joy.

   Why does James tell his readers to celebrate trials?

2. There are many kinds of tests: actual persecution, which many face today; fierce and nasty temptations, which can strike suddenly when we're not expecting them; physical sickness or bereavement; family or financial troubles; and so on. But you wouldn't be tested unless you were doing something serious. Mechanics don't test scrap metal; they test cars that are going to face tough conditions. Those who follow Jesus the Messiah are not simply supposed to survive. They are supposed to count, to make a difference in the world, whether through the quiet daily witness of a faithful and gentle life or the chance, given to some, to speak and act in a way which reveals the gospel to many others. For all of that we need to become strong, to face up to the challenge.

   How can letting patience have its full effect result in our being whole and complete, not lacking anything (v. 4)?

3. When has patience had a positive effect on you and your life as the result of the testing of your faith?

4. Wisdom is needed to cope with trials and to build patience. Why does James emphasize asking for wisdom with faith (vv. 5-8)?

5. What does James stress about God in this passage that makes us able to ask for wisdom with such hopeful expectation?

6. How is James's view of God different from common understandings (or misunderstandings!) of what God is like?

7. How can having a wrong view of God result in doubting God?

8. What does James say will happen when we ask for wisdom yet doubt that God will give it (v. 6)?

9. When have you experienced receiving wisdom that you asked for?

10. The challenge of faith is the challenge not to be a wave. There are many winds and tides in human life, and it's easy to imagine ourselves important because we seem, from time to time at least, to dance and sparkle this way and that. The question is whether the character that develops within us is the real thing, or whether, as James says in verse 6, we are simply double-minded and unstable, blown and tossed about by this wind or that.

In what ways has life tossed you about?

11. Learning who God really is and what he is truly like—and reminding ourselves of it regularly—is the key to it all. Without that we will be double-minded, swept this way one minute and that way the next. We'll just be another wave. With it, you will have a settled character. Wisdom. Patience. Faith.

As you consider this passage, what steps would you like to take to grow in the character and faith that come from knowing God?

PRAY

Knowing that God is at the core of this passage, ask him to open your heart to him and to help you know him better.

Thank him for giving generously and unbegrudgingly to you.

Ask him to help you grow in faith and patience and trust as you know him better.

Ask the Holy Spirit to give you the wisdom that he so freely offers.

2

The Snares of the World and the Gift of God

James 1:9-18

Listen for the echo," said my friend. We were standing at the back of a great cathedral, and the choir was about to sing a powerful, beautiful anthem. Sure enough: the conductor knew what he was doing. As each part of the anthem developed, the building seemed to pick it up, cherish it, play with it and use it as the background to the next part. After a while it was hard to tell what was actual echo and what was in our memory, in our mind, while we were listening to the next bit.

When, finally, the choir fell silent, there was a full ten seconds in which we could savor the last chord. The whole building was designed that way, so as to give the impression that, along with the human choir, there were other, older voices, hundreds of years of worship on earth, joining in. Not to mention the heavenly host themselves.

OPEN

Some echoes are wonderful while others are annoying. What experiences have you had listening to echoes?

STUDY

1. *Read James 1:9-18.* In this passage James warns his readers to avoid two snares. The first snare is wealth. In light of this snare, why are the poor called to celebrate (vv. 9-11)?

2. Listen for the echo! The early Christians lived and worked within a massive echo chamber, more vast than any cathedral. It was, of course, the Old Testament. In this text we find a clear echo of a famous passage the prophet Isaiah wrote in chapter 40, verse 8. "The grass withers, the flower fades, but the word of our God will stand forever" (ESV). James is encouraging us to hear the particular teaching he is giving within this much larger echo chamber, to allow the ancient echoes to color the way we think about what he's saying.

    Why are the rich to celebrate when they are brought low?

3. In what ways do you put your confidence in your wealth or possessions?

4. How does wealth or poverty affect your relationship with God?

5. The second snare James speaks of is temptation. (The two snares often go together, of course, as when someone is tempted to cheat or steal to

become rich.) Where does James say temptation comes from (v. 14)?

6. What is the result of succumbing to temptation (v. 15)?

7. In stark contrast to death, the end result of temptation, God promises the crown of life to those who endure. How can you recognize that you are being tempted, in order to avoid succumbing to it?

8. In verses 16-18 James once again focuses on the true character of God, warning us not to be deceived by wrong ideas. How is God described in verses 17 and 18?

9. What difference should it make to us that we have this kind of God when we are faced with the attraction of wealth or other temptations?

10. The question James raises is, What is going to last? What is permanent? His answer is clear: God and his Word. What James is saying in this passage is that we must learn to trust God and his Word rather than the snares of the world.

How can this Word of God also protect from various temptations?

11. When God speaks, things happen. Things happen *to us*. Things happen *in us*. The Word of God is like medicine which goes down deep inside, healing our inner hurts and changing our inner motivations, so that we actually become different people (v. 18). How have you experienced the Word of God working healing and change in you?

12. Where in your life do you need the Word of God now to heal hurts or change motivations?

PRAY

Sit in silence before the Lord.

Listen to the echo of his voice.

Reflect on the truth about God we have considered in this passage.

Praise him for being a generous giver, the father of lights. That he is constant.

Praise him that one day, his Word will transform the whole creation, filling heaven and earth with his rich, wonderful light and life.

Ask him to reveal to you and then change the inner motivations in you that are not pleasing to him.

Thank him for the fruit he is producing in you.

NOTE ON JAMES 1:13

In particular, recognize what's happening when you are tempted. Developing what James said about trials and tribulations in verse 2, he warns us not to imagine that God is responsible for the temptation itself. The testing comes from within (Jesus made that clear too). None of us starts off with a pure internal "kit" of impulses, hopes and fears. If you are true to "yourself" you will end up a complete mess. The challenge is to take the "self" you find within, and to choose wisely which impulses and desires to follow, and which ones to resist.

NOTE ON JAMES 1:15

Some desires, says James, start a family tree of their own. Desire is like a woman who conceives a child, and the child is sin: the act which flows directly from that part of the "self" which pulls us away from the genuine life which God has for us. And when the child, sin, grows up and becomes mature, it too has a child. That child is death: the final result of following those desires which diminish that genuine human life. The contrast could hardly be sharper: God promises "the crown of life" (v. 12), but those desires lead in exactly the opposite direction. Here, as so often in Scripture, the teaching of "wisdom" fits together with what the ancient Israelites saw as God's covenant promise, requiring the choice between life and death.

NOTE ON JAMES 1:18

Those in whose lives the Word is doing its work are just the start. We, says James, are "a kind of first fruits of his creatures." Another echo, this time of the early harvest festival in the temple. You bring the "first fruits," the beginning of the crop, as an offering to God, as a sign that there is much more to come. One day, God's Word will transform the whole creation, filling heaven and earth with his rich, wonderful light and life. Our lives, transformed by the gospel, learning to look at the world differently, standing firm against temptation, are just the start of that larger project.

THE WORD THAT
GOES TO WORK

James 1:19-27

Human wisdom regularly produces proverbs. "A stitch in time saves nine." "A rolling stone gathers no moss." And so on. One of the proverbs I learned very early in life went like this: "Sticks and stones may break my bones, but words will never hurt me." I think we boys at school used to chant it to one another as a response to a silly playground insult.

But of course that proverb is very misleading. You can recover from a broken leg or arm. But if someone smears your good name—if someone tells lies about you, and other people believe them—it may be much, much harder. You may never get the job you want. People may never quite trust you. Friends, even family, may turn away. Words can be terrible things. They can leave lasting wounds.

OPEN

What proverbs or common sayings have been a part of your family and culture?

STUDY

1. *Read James 1:19-27.* Here James introduces another of his key themes: the dangerous power of the human tongue. What clear directives does James give in verse 19?

2. How have you found these three directives interrelated in your own experience?

3. In this passage we see a theme which many early Christian writers emphasized: the danger of human anger. James has been emphasizing the need for patience; anger is, of course, one of the things that happens when patience reaches its limit. We always imagine that when the world is out of joint, a bit of our own anger will put things straight. What results have you experienced when you tried to make things right through your anger?

4. According to verses 20 and 21, what are we told to do to avoid the human anger that doesn't produce God's justice?

5. The way God works in us and through us is not by taking our nasty or malicious anger to somehow make things right. The way God

works is, again, through his Word. But how does this happen? Every generation in the church worries, rightly, about people who just glide along, seeming to enjoy what they hear in church but without it making any real difference. "Nominal Christians," we sometimes say. It is comforting, in a way, to know that James faced exactly the same problem in the very first generation: people who were happy to listen to the Word (this presumably means both the teaching of the Old Testament and the message about Jesus) but who went away without it having affected them very much.

Here he uses an interesting illustration. In his day there were, of course, no photographs. Hardly anyone had their portrait painted. Not many people possessed mirrors, either. So if you did happen to catch sight of yourself, you might well forget at once what you looked like. That's what it's like, says James, for some when they hear God's Word. A quick glance—"Oh, yes," they think, "that's interesting"—and then they forget it straight away and carry on as before.

When and why are you apt to take just a "quick glance" at the Word?

6. What does it mean to receive the Word humbly (v. 21)?

7. When have you been blessed by *doing* the Word of God?

8. James reminds us that Scripture, and the message about Jesus, really is "the perfect law of freedom." How can a law create freedom? (Or think of it another way: if there were no laws, how would that actually restrict the way people live?)

9. James is nothing if not practical. After this flash of glorious theology he comes back to earth with a bump. A pious person with a foul mouth is a contradiction in terms (v. 26). Such people are deceiving themselves—but no one else. What damage have you seen done to the cause of Christ because of the tongue?

10. When is it difficult for you to keep a tight rein on your tongue, and how do you seek to do so?

11. James doesn't immediately say what the remedy to the tongue is but he says, in effect, "All right: you want to follow in God's way? Here's how! There are people out there who need your help; and there is a messy world out there that will try to mess up your life as well. Make sure you focus on the first and avoid the second." Good brief teaching. Almost like a set of proverbs.

Think about your life—the pace of it, the people you interact with, the activities you're involved in. What is one change you could make this week to help you focus more on those in need?

12. James also reminds his readers in verse 27 that true devotion to God includes helping those in need (such as widows and orphans) and not being stained by the world. How do these two dimensions offer a balanced view of the Christian life?

PRAY

If what we want is God's justice, coming to sort things out, we will do better to get entirely out of the way and let God do his own work, rather than supposing our burst of anger (which will most likely have all sorts of nasty bits to it, such as wounded pride, malice and envy) will somehow help God do what needs to be done.

Talk to your heavenly Father about situations in which anger erupts in your life.

Pray that he will build patience and grace in you as well as the ability to trust him to make things right.

Ask him for mercy and grace to speak only in ways that bring pleasure and glory to him.

NOTE ON JAMES 1:25

James has a remedy for a quick glance at the Word which is soon forgotten. He reminds us what the word of Scripture, and the message about Jesus, really is: it is "the perfect law of freedom." To us that sounds like a contradiction in terms. How can a "law" be part of "freedom"? Isn't a law something which restricts your freedom, which stops you doing what you want?

Yes and no. Supposing we didn't have a law about which side of the road we were supposed to drive on. Everyone would set off and do their own thing. It would be chaos: accidents, near-misses and nobody able to go at any speed for fear of disaster. The law that says you drive on the left (in Britain and elsewhere) or the right (in America and elsewhere) sets you free. That's what God's law is like: by restricting your "freedom' in some ways, it opens up far greater, genuine freedoms in all other ways. And the point is this: when you look into this "law," the Word of God, it is supposed to change you. The word must go to work. When that happens, God's blessing—that is, God's enrichment of your life in all kinds of new ways—will surely follow.

No Favorites

James 2:1-13

I have often been embarrassed in church, but one of the worst moments was on Easter morning many years ago. I had arrived at the service in what I thought was good time, but there was already a large queue outside and it wasn't moving. Clearly the place was already packed. I was wondering what to do when a familiar voice greeted me. I turned round and saw a man I knew a bit, a very senior and distinguished person in the city. I was flattered to be recognized and singled out. But then came the moment. "Come with me," he said conspiratorially. He led me forward, past the queue, to one of the ushers.

"I am Lord Smith," he said to the man (I use "Smith," of course, as a pseudonym). "I would be grateful if you could find my friend and myself somewhere to sit."

Before I had time to think, the two of us were escorted right to the front of the church, where we were given excellent seats.

OPEN

Describe a time when you were on the receiving end of favoritism or showed favoritism to someone else.

STUDY

1. *Read James 2:1-13.* In verse 1 James states clearly that we must practice the faith of the Lord Jesus, the anointed king of glory, without favoritism. What example does he give of showing favoritism (vv. 2-3)?

2. According to verses 4-6, what are the results of practicing favoritism?

Despite the excellent seat with a full view of the Easter service at the church I mentioned above, I did not enjoy it. I was thinking about this passage and wondering if either my acquaintance or the usher had read it recently. This passage simply rules out any question of pulling social rank in church. This is part of what James means at the end of the previous chapter by not letting the world leave its dirty smudge on you.

3. We often hear the phrase "God's upside-down kingdom," meaning that God acts in ways opposite to how the world tends to act. What upside-down value do you see in verse 5?

The world is always assessing people, sizing them up, putting them down, establishing a pecking order. And God, who sees and loves all alike, wants the church to reflect his generous, universal love in how it behaves. In some parts of the early church they had a rule that if a regular member of the congregation came into church the usher would look after them, but that if a stranger came in, particularly a poor stranger, the bishop himself would leave his chair and go to the door to welcome the newcomer. I have often wished I had the courage to do that.

4. When have you or your Christian community failed to obey God in practicing equality of treatment?

5. According to verses 5-7, why is it ridiculous to dishonor the poor?

6. And why (according to James and as seen in life today) is it often equally ridiculous to honor the rich?

7. In contrast is the royal law of Jesus. What is this royal law?

8. Contrast the results of keeping the royal law with not keeping it (vv. 8-11).

9. How does breaking one law make a person guilty of breaking the whole royal law?

10. What would it mean in your life to act like one who is going to be judged by the law of freedom (v. 12)?

11. Explain what James means in verse 13 when he writes that judgment is without mercy to those who have shown no mercy.

12. When have you seen mercy triumph over judgment?

Here is the paradox, to which James returns in verse 13. God's mercy is sovereign. It will triumph. But the minute you say "Oh well, that's all right then; God will forgive, so it doesn't matter what I do"—and, in particular, when "what I do" includes discriminating against the poor—then, precisely because God is the God of mercy, he must act in judgment. He will not forever tolerate a world in which mercy is not the ultimate rule of life.

"Mercy" isn't the same as a shoulder-shrugging "tolerance," an "anything goes" attitude to life. "Anything" doesn't "go." "Anything" includes arrogance, corruption, blasphemy, favoritism and lawbreaking of all kinds. If God was "merciful" to that lot, he would be deeply *unmerciful* to the poor, the helpless, the innocent and the victims. And the whole gospel insists that in precisely those cases his mercy shines out most particularly. So must ours.

PRAY

Ask the Lord to reveal to you the ways in which you break his royal law. Confess your need for his cleansing. Pray about the steps he wants you to take to follow his mandate to "love your neighbor as yourself."

Pray for the poor and needy throughout the world. Ask God to lead you in ways to be involved in caring for the poor. Ask him to make you sensitive to the tendency that you might have to honor some people above others.

NOTE ON JAMES 2:7

James hints that the rich are likely to be oppressors, and even persecutors of the church. In every society, unless it takes scrupulous care, the rich can operate the "justice" system to their own advantage. They can hire the best lawyers; they can, perhaps, even bribe the judges. They can get their way, and the poor have to put up with it. And in James's society "the rich" may be more sinister still. As verse 7 indicates, in the first century it was most likely "the rich" who were anxious about the dangers of this new messianic movement. These raggle-taggle Jesus-followers, making a fuss about an executed madman, were thinking that God's new world had already been born, upsetting the power structures of the day. And that might not prove to be so good for those enjoying privilege in the present world!

NOTE ON JAMES 2:8

Jesus has reemphasized one of the most central passages of Israel's ancient law: "Love your neighbor as yourself." That was central to Jesus' teaching (Matthew 22:36-40), and it remained central in early Christianity. But it needed to be spelled out and applied, as here, to one situation after another. This is the "royal law," by which James presumably means "the law which King Jesus himself endorsed and insists upon." This passage, incidentally, is one of several which make it quite clear that the early church really did see Jesus as "king," as "Messiah." They believed that God had established his "kingdom" in and through Jesus, and they were determined to live under that rule, whether or not the rest of the world—and the rest of the Jewish people whose Messiah Jesus was!—took any notice.

FAITH AND WORKS

James 2:14-26

In this study we'll look at one of the most well-known verses in the whole letter of James: "Just as the body without the spirit is dead, you see, so faith without works is dead." But isn't that the wrong way round? If we were to use "the body and the spirit" as a picture for "faith and works," wouldn't we make "faith" correspond to the "spirit" and "works" to the "body"? After all, faith happens in the spiritual dimension, and works in the bodily dimension, don't they? But James does the opposite. Here we'll be seeking to sort out what James has in mind.

OPEN

How are you affected when a person says they care about you deeply but there are no actions behind his or her words?

STUDY

1. *Read James 2:14-26.* James is very concerned about a problem which was already arising in the earliest church and which is with us to this day. He has already begun to address this problem in the previ-

ous chapter, when he spoke about being "people who do the word, not merely people who hear it." He has heard people talking about "faith," not meaning a rich, lively trust in the loving, living God, but rather a shell, a husk, an empty affirmation, a bare acknowledgment.

In verses 14-17, how does James illustrate faith that is like a body without a spirit?

2. What examples can you think of that similarly illustrate an empty faith?

3. Actually verses 15 and 16 don't just provide an "illustration" of the fact that faith without works is dead. As we see throughout the letter, one of the key "works" that James expects followers of Jesus to do is to care for the poor.

    What are ways that you are caring or could begin to care for the poor?

4. How does giving of ourselves for the poor demonstrate faith?

5. In verse 19 James goes back to one of the most basic points of ancient Judaism, the confession that "God is one." That was, and still is, at the heart of Jewish daily prayer found in Deuteronomy 6:4-5:

"Hear, O Israel: the LORD our God, the LORD is One; and you shall love the LORD your God with all your heart, and mind, and soul and strength." It was at that point that Jesus himself added what James has earlier called "the royal law," "Love your neighbor as yourself" (Matthew 22:36-40).

But simply saying "God is one" doesn't get you very far if it doesn't make a difference in your life. After all, as James points out, the demons know all this too, and it doesn't do them any good; it merely scares them out of their wits. So it becomes clear that what James means by *faith* in this passage is not what Paul and others developed as a full, Jesus-shaped meaning; it is the basic *ancient Jewish* meaning, the confession of God as "one." This, he says, needs to translate into action, into Jesus-shaped action, if it is to make any significant difference. At this point, he is actually on the same page as Paul, who in his fiercest letter about faith and works defines "what matters" as "faith working through love" (Galatians 5:6).

According to verses 18-20, why is faith without works considered dead faith?

6. James mentions two famous people in Scripture. The first is Abraham, the father of the Israelite people (vv. 21-24). James brings together two key passages: one is Genesis 15, where Abraham believes in God's promise to give him an enormous family even though he is childless. The other passage is Genesis 22. There, following the awful episode about Abraham fathering a son on his slave-girl Hagar, and then sending them away, Abraham faces a stern test. He is commanded to sacrifice Isaac, his son by Sarah, the son through whom those great promises were to be fulfilled. It's a dark episode, but Abraham proceeds as told, with God stopping him at the last moment and providing a ram to sacrifice instead.

How do you see Abraham's faith cooperating with his works in both instances?

7. How does James then characterize Abraham's relationship with God in 2:23?

8. In what ways would you like to grow as a "friend of God"?

That friendship, embodied in the "covenant" which God established in Genesis 15:7-21 and reaffirmed in 22:15-18, is the basis for what James, like Paul, calls "justification," God's declaration that a person is a member of the covenant, is "in the right," is part of God's forgiven family.

9. The second person James mentions is Rahab. His Jewish audience would have recognized her immediately. She appears, initially, to be an unlikely example of faith, since she was a pagan prostitute. She lived in the city of Jericho at the time when the Israelites, on their way to the Promised Land, were about to cross the river Jordan with Jericho as their first target. In the story, Joshua sent two men, ahead of his invasion, to spy out the city. They stayed the night in Rahab's house. She hid them from the troops who were looking for them, explaining that she had come to believe in Israel's God as the only true God in heaven and earth (Joshua 2:11).

    In return, Joshua spared her and her family when the invasion took place. She seems to have married an Israelite, and became, remarkably enough, the great-great-grandmother of King David, and hence part of the family tree of Jesus himself (Matthew 1:5).

What are the similarities and differences between Abraham and Rahab?

10. As you consider this passage, how do you want to grow as a person of faith that is demonstrated and fulfilled by a life of works?

11. Think again about the observation at the beginning of this study that it seems as though James got it turned around when he compared faith to the body and works to the spirit. How does this last part of chapter 2 help us understand how works enliven faith?

PRAY

Ask the Holy Spirit to reveal to you where in your life and experience your faith needs to translate into action.

Sit quietly and listen to what he says.

Now talk to God about the steps you want to take to live a full, Jesus-shaped faith.

6

TAMING THE TONGUE

James 3:1-18

Some while ago I was asked to give a talk about my early life and why I had chosen the path I did. I was surprised, when preparing the talk, to discover how many of the key moments in my first fifteen years had to do with my teachers. Like many others, I suppose, I had some good teachers and some bad ones; but among the good ones there were two or three who took the trouble to get to know me, to find out what made me tick, and to give me friendly words of encouragement and advice. Often that's all it takes. Someone you trust says one or two sentences, and a door opens into a whole new world.

OPEN

How have one or two teachers had a significant impact on you, perhaps even affecting directions you've taken in life?

STUDY

1. *Read James 3:1-12.* Having begun with a somber warning about how difficult it is to come up to the mark as a teacher, James expands the

point: taming the tongue in general, for anyone, is so difficult as to be almost impossible. Get that right and you've obviously got your entire self under control. The tongue, it seems, is the last bit of a human being to learn its lesson.

How does James say in verses 3-4 that the tongue is like a bit and a rudder?

2. We know only too well how the tongue is a fire (v. 5), ready to set things ablaze, from the way the media eagerly trips up politicians and other public figures. We know that one word out of place can ruin a career or bring down a government. One unwise remark, reported and circulated on the Internet, can cause riots on the other side of the world. So, says James, the tongue is like a little world all of its own, a country within a country: the larger area, the person as a whole, may be well governed, but in this smaller region corruption and wickedness reign unchecked.

When have you seen or experienced significant damage caused by a few words?

3. How does James explain the outrageousness of the inconsistencies of the tongue (vv. 9-12)?

4. What James is after, then, is consistency. He wants people to follow Jesus through and through, to be blessing-only people rather than blessing-and-cursing people. It's a high standard, but we should expect no less if the gospel is indeed the message of salvation. The danger, as always, is that people will take the bits of the message they want, and quietly leave the real challenges to one side. But it can't be done. The spring must be cleansed so that only fresh, sweet water comes out. For this we need help. That, fortunately, is what the gospel offers.

    In what specific ways could you bless friends, enemies, family, co-workers, fellow Christians or those of other beliefs more consistently?

5. How does this passage motivate you to be more careful about how you use your tongue?

6. *Read James 3:13-18.* Why does James connect humility and wisdom?

7. How does James distinguish the wisdom that is earthly and the wisdom that comes from demons?

8. When have you experienced the results of bitter jealousy and contention within a Christian community? Within yourself?

9. It is no accident that James follows his teaching on the tongue with teaching on true and false wisdom. When he talks about "bitter jealousy and contention," a spirit which is always carping and criticizing, he speaks of one which cannot let a nice word go by without adding a nasty one. This problem goes deeper. He has already said that the tongue is a fire set aflame by hell; now he says that a mindset like that comes from the world of demons.

   How might such an attitude of cynicism give the appearance of wisdom?

10. The challenge for God's people that James lays out in verse 17 is to be able to tell the truth about the way the world is, and about the way wicked people are behaving, without turning into a perpetual grumble, and in particular without becoming someone whose appearance of "wisdom" consists in being able to find a cutting word to say about everyone and everything.

   Offer some examples of speaking in a way that lights a candle rather than curses the darkness.

11. Why would this wisdom that comes from above produce the fruit of righteousness that is sown in peace?

12. What needs to happen for this fruit of righteousness that is sown in peace to thrive in your community?

PRAY

James paints a picture of the tongue and the evil that comes from it. He takes the tongue seriously and says that it is impossible for us to tame our tongue. He also describes the horror of false wisdom and the beauty of true wisdom. Ask the Holy Spirit to impress upon you the sin and the damage that comes from your tongue. Now confess the sins to God that the Holy Spirit has brought to your mind.

Talk to him about the "false wisdom" in you.

Take time now to work slowly, one by one, through the characteristics of true wisdom that James mentions. Review your life in light of them.

Humbly ask the Holy Spirit to grow in you true wisdom.

Finally, praise God for his love and forgiveness and for the fact that you are always invited to turn to him to be forgiven.

NOTE ON JAMES 3:5-12

These verses bring home the real underlying point. Why is the tongue like this? Jesus had pointed out that what comes out of the mouth is a sign of what is really there, deep in the heart (Matthew 12:34/Luke 6:45). James echoes this passage when he speaks of the fig tree bearing olives or the vine bearing figs. Things just aren't like that! If someone is pouring out curses—cursing other humans who are made in God's likeness—then one must at least question whether his or her heart has been properly cleansed, rinsed by God's powerful Spirit. And if that isn't the case, it turns out that the tongue isn't simply a private world of injustice. It is getting its real inspiration from hell itself (v. 6).

7

Humility and Faith

James 4:1-17

Schoolchildren of a certain age form exclusive friendships. Great human dramas are played out on a small scale when your daughter comes home in tears because her "best friend" has declared she isn't her best friend any more, but has taken up with someone else. It seems for a moment like the end of the world. Such crises are often short-lived, not least because children grow out of that phase of life and learn to make friends more widely, and on a variety of levels.

But in other respects exclusivity is the very essence of a relationship. The obvious example is marriage. In the Bible, the exclusive partnership of marriage is often used as an image of the exclusive claims of God on the human life, and so it is here in James 4.

OPEN

What are some of the benefits of the exclusive relationship in marriage?

STUDY

1. *Read James 4:1-17.* What explanation for fighting and waging wars does James give in this passage?

2. James doesn't call some of his readers "adulterers" (vv. 4-5) to accuse them of actual unfaithfulness in their marriages. What's he trying to communicate?

3. By "the world" James seems to mean, as often is the case in Scripture, "the way the world behaves," the pattern of life, the underlying implicit story, the things people want, expect, long for and dream of that drive them to think and behave the way they do. If you go with the drift, if you don't reflect on what you're doing but just pick up habits of mind and body from all around you, the chances are you will become "friends" with "the world" in this sense. You will be "normal." It takes guts to stand out and be different. It also takes thought, decision and determination.

   What are some patterns or values of the world that are easy to drift along and accept without much thought that might actually be in conflict with a biblical perspective?

4. At the heart of this challenge to be a friend of God there lies a double promise so stupendous that I suspect most of us never really take it seriously. To begin with, "resist the devil and he will run away from you" (v. 7). The devil is a coward; when he is resisted, with the prayer that claims the victory of Jesus on the cross, he knows he is beaten. His trick is to whisper that we know we can't resist; he's got us before and he'll get us again, so why not just give in straight away and save all that bother? It's a lie. Resist him and he will run.

What are practical ways you can resist the devil?

5. James then contrasts resisting the devil with this promise: "Draw near to God, and he will draw near to you" (v. 8). That is astonishing! God is ready and waiting. He longs to establish a friendship with you, a friendship deeper, stronger and more satisfying than you can ever imagine.

   Why is it sometimes hard to believe that God actually wants this kind of relationship with us?

6. James sandwiches his advice on resisting the devil, drawing near to God and having pure hearts between comments on humility in verses 6 and 10. Apparently humility has something to do with these directions. What is the connection?

7. In verses 11 and 12 James warns about speaking evil of one another. He seems to have in mind the kind of slander or gossip which eats its way like a cancer in a Christian fellowship, and requires urgent treatment if it is not to prove fatal. His point is this: anyone who does such a thing is thereby implying that the ordinary "law" which applies to Christians—that they should love their neighbor as they love themselves—does not apply to them. They are above it! They can look down on such petty standards from a great height! They are, says James, "judging the law," instead of trying to do what the law says.

When are people tempted to think they are "above the law" (whether the laws of the land or of Scripture) and why?

8. Why is it so easy to talk about what's wrong with other people and cast them in a bad light?

9. Throughout this passage James warns against the temptation to put yourself in the place of God. How do verses 13-16 highlight this danger in relation to our future plans?

10. James again has stern words in store. Don't you realize, he says, what your life is like? Think of the mist you see out of the window on an autumn morning. It hangs there in the valley, above the little stream. It is beautiful, evocative, mysterious; yes, just like a human being can be. Then the sun comes up a bit further, and . . . the mist simply disappears. That's what your life is like. You have no idea what today will bring, let alone tomorrow.

How do you respond to James's observation about the fragility of your life?

11. In practical terms, what would it look like to live out an attitude that expresses, "If the Lord wills, we shall live, and we shall do this, or that"?

12. The chapter ends with a warning which is far more general, and indeed far more worrying, than what has gone before. Not to do what you know you should do is actually to sin! It isn't enough to avoid the obvious acts of sin. Once you learn the humility to accept God's royal law and to live by it, to accept God's sovereign ordering of all life and to live within that, then you will see more clearly the positive things to which you are being called. This may be a major life-decision, a question of your whole vocation and path of life. Or it may be the small Spirit-given nudge to do a small act of kindness for a neighbor or stranger. But once you have had that nudge, that call, then to ignore it, to pretend you hadn't heard, is a further act of pride, setting yourself up in the place of God.

As you look over this passage, in what ways is God calling or nudging you to do what you know is right?

PRAY

As you sit in silence read James 4:1-17. Ask the Holy Spirit to reveal to you how you are a friend of the world.

Talk to the Lord about your friendship with the world.

The cure, of course, of being a friend with the world is to submit to God and resist the devil. This may well mean a time of serious self-examination. Where are all these impulses coming from, these desires that are pulling me away from the God who truly longs to be my friend? Verses 8-10 (drawing near to God, cleansing hands and hearts, mourning and humility) sound to me like an agenda for at least six months of spiritual direction, or perhaps for an extended silent retreat. "The world" will do its best to encourage you to play at doing these things. Five minutes of drawing near to God, and then quickly back to two hours of television. A brief cleansing of the hands and then back to the mud and the muck. A short, painful glance at the depths of the heart, and then we'll decide that that had better wait for another occasion. After all, we don't want to be gloomy, do we? Doesn't God want us to be joyful?

Talk to the Lord about specific ways that you want to resist the devil and specific ways that you want to submit to God.

Now thank God that he is God and you are not.

NOTE ON JAMES 4:17

This closing verse has sometimes produced, in sensitive souls, a continual anguish of heart-searching: am I being disloyal or disobedient? Can I be sure I've done what I ought to do? The best thing to say about that is that if you're worried on that score—and frankly I wish a few more Christians would search their hearts in that way—then the chances are you are doing fine. To worry obsessively about it, actually, may in itself be a way of putting yourself in the middle of the picture, focusing all the attention on "me and my state of mind and heart" rather than on God and on your neighbor. Of course, some people do suffer from pathological or paranoid heart-searching, and that requires more careful pastoral help. But for most of us, there's nothing like helping someone else in their troubles for putting our own internal worries in perspective.

8

THE RICH AND
THE SUFFERING

James 5:1-12

Whaen my sister and I were reckoned to be old enough not to need a babysitter any more, my parents occasionally went out for the evening, leaving us on our own. Normally this worked fine. We could see to ourselves, the front door was locked, and in any case the world seemed a safer place in those days. But one evening, for some reason, I began to worry. I have no idea why, but instead of going to sleep as usual I stayed awake and fretted. Supposing something had happened to them? What if there had been an accident? Perhaps they wouldn't come, not that night, not ever? I think my sister must have been asleep by then, because she would have told me not to be silly, but I ended up sitting by the window, cold with fear, hardly able to believe it when eventually the car turned up our road, stopped, and there were my parents safe and sound after a good evening, and puzzled that I would have been anxious.

I suspect that when Jesus finally appears many of us will have the same sense as I did then: how could we have been so foolish as to doubt it? How could we think that, just because it was later than we had wanted and hoped, it might mean he would never come at all? Every generation of Christians has prayed that he would come, as he promised, and so far every generation has had to learn the lesson of patience that James offers.

OPEN

What have you had difficulty being patient for recently?

STUDY

1. *Read James 5:1-6.* Why, according to James, should the rich weep and wail?

2. "You have stored up riches," warns James in verse 3, "*in the last days.*" James believed that with Jesus, God's new world had begun! He had launched God's kingdom, on earth as in heaven: this is "the age to come" for which Israel had longed and prayed! These are, in that sense, "the last days," the great new time in which everything would be set right at last.

   This is one of the sharpest warnings against careless luxury anywhere in the Bible. Why do you think that James took the fact that they "stored up riches in the last days" so seriously?

3. Withholding fair wages from laborers may seem remote to us (v. 4). But even today in many countries of the world, including the Western world, the gap between the richest 5 percent and the lowest 80 percent continues to widen inordinately. We may be weary of saying

it and hearing it, but the way the global economy is set up is designed to produce more or less the same effect as the ancient Judean economy, with most of the money flowing steadily in one direction. This is reproduced again and again more locally, as small groups of powerful people make sure they possess not just "enough," but more than enough—and then more again—while others struggle, go bankrupt and lack basic services.

No doubt, like the Jerusalem elite, the rich will then pour scorn on the poor: they deserve it, they're lazy, they don't know what life is all about. But the church must keep James 5:1-6 at its elbow, and must continue to speak out against the wickedness, not only individual but also systemic, that colludes with such a situation.

What should the church do and say about the wrong way riches are handled individually and in society as a whole?

4. Wealth is always a relative thing. We can always think of people who have more than we do, and so excuse ourselves from the accusation of being one of those "rich people." How can we overcome this problem and gain an accurate perspective on our actual situation when it comes to how rich or poor we are?

5. James meant his readers to take his comments generally about wealth and poverty with deadly seriousness. And we should as well. Besides having the rich in general in mind, he also had one particular group in view. In verse 6 he says, "You have condemned the Righteous One and killed him, and he doesn't resist you." "The rich" are the Jerusalem elite—the Sadducees and the chief priests—who live in their fine

houses and grow fat on the proceeds of pilgrimages and sacrifices brought by faithful Jews, but whose attitude to God and his law is purely pragmatic. Doing what's required in the temple, running the liturgy and the festivals the way the people expect, is simply their way of staying in power. Their job is to keep the peace for the Romans, by force if necessary; and that means keeping a tight hold on what happens in Judea, and in particular in Jerusalem and the temple itself.

How do power and wealth work hand in hand in our world today as well?

6. What warnings in this passage do you see as being relevant to you?

7. *Read James 5:7-12.* In verse 7 James urges patience as we await the coming of Christ. At the beginning of this study I mentioned how generations of Christians have waited for Jesus to appear again. How would you describe what it is like for you to wait for the return of the Lord?

8. In contrast to James's warnings about careless luxury in the first five verses of this chapter, how does James encourage his readers to be patient for the appearing of the Lord (vv. 7-9)?

9. A hasty spirit is another form of pride. Once again James writes about speech. How should being patient affect our speech (v. 9)?

10. How are the prophets and Job examples of patience (vv. 10-11)?

11. Focus on God is what makes it possible to have strong hearts and to be patient. What do you see of God in this passage which will help you to be patient as you wait for the Lord's return?

12. What aspects of God that you see here should you focus on and why?

PRAY

Praise God for what you have seen of him in this passage.

Confess to the Lord your greed and hoarding of riches and ask him to make you into a person who knows and lives out, with your possessions, the truth that Jesus is coming soon.

Pray for God to have mercy on a world where the rich become richer and more oppressive and the poor become poorer.

Pray that the church of Jesus Christ would speak and act against such greed and oppression.

Ask God for patience in the midst of troubles as you await the Lord's return to put all things right.

NOTE ON JAMES 5:9 AND 12

The repeated warnings about the coming judgment have now developed from the general truth stated in the early chapters (for example, 2:8-13) into a more specific warning about the coming day of the Lord. "The judge is standing at the gates!" (v. 9). It is possible, James insists again, to incur that judgment by the wrong kind of speech. How easy it is to add a few words to a statement, as though to strengthen it. To add an oath would mean, if taken literally, that we were invoking some supernatural power in support of what we were saying ("I swear by God," and so forth). This remains a solemn matter in a court of law, and the crime of perjury is still regarded as extremely serious, even in a secular world where most people don't actually believe in the "God" by whom, officially, they are swearing. But James, once more following the teaching of his older brother (Matthew 5:34-37), insists that saying "yes" and "no" is quite enough. Anything more risks invoking not divine support, but divine judgment.

This has, of course, been controversial, because many countries still use an oath in a court of law as a way of guaranteeing truthful testimony. Many Christians believe that that is a "special case" in which the normal rule, as here, doesn't apply. But that controversy shouldn't blind us to the very interesting point that lies behind the teaching of both James and Jesus here. Following Jesus is supposed to be the path to a genuine human existence, and genuine human life should issue in clear, straight, honest speaking. To add oaths or other similar embellishments to what we are saying has the effect of debasing the coinage. It makes it look as though a plain statement isn't enough. The one time we are told in the Bible that someone began to curse and swear was when Peter was insisting that he didn't know Jesus. That should give us pause for thought.

PRAYING IN FAITH

James 5:13-20

There are many things in life which look extremely odd to someone who doesn't know what's going on. Imagine watching someone making a musical instrument if you'd never heard music in your life. What, you might think, can such an object possibly be for? Why waste such time and effort on it? Or imagine a child, who has no idea about babies and where they come from, or of the fact that his mother is expecting one soon, watching her get the room ready for the new arrival. It makes no sense. Why this little cot? Why these new decorations?

Of course, when the moment comes, all is explained. But sometimes you have to wait, to be patient (that theme again), to trust that things will come clear. James has used other examples too, the farmer and the harvest being the obvious one. This theme of patience, which has run through the whole letter, marks his thinking out from the ordinary moralism of his day. James is constantly aware of living within a story—living, in fact, within God's story—and of the fact that this story has already reached its climax in his brother Jesus and will one day complete what he had so solidly begun.

This is the setting within which prayer, that most incomprehensible of activities, makes sense.

OPEN

How does prayer both make sense and at the same time seem incomprehensible?

STUDY

1. *Read James 5:13-20.* To someone with no idea of God, with no idea of there being a world other than what we can touch and see, prayer looks at best like an odd superstition and at worst like serious self-deception. Fancy just talking to yourself and thinking it will make a difference to anything! But almost all human traditions, right across history and culture, have been aware of other dimensions which seem mysteriously to intersect with our own. The ancient Jewish tradition, which comes to fresh and vital expression in Jesus himself and in his early followers and family, sharpens up this general vague awareness of Something Else into not only Someone Else but a named Someone: the God we know in, through and as Jesus himself. Then, suddenly, prayer, and the patience which it involves, make all the sense in the world.

    Why is it quite appropriate for James to finish this letter with a call to prayer?

2. What instructions does James give to his readers in verses 13-14?

3. What are the results of following these instructions (v. 15)?

4. How is each result mysterious and full of meaning?

5. How do you respond to the promise that prayer offered in faith for the sick will make them well?

6. Why do you think James connects healing with forgiveness?

7. Forgiveness is there, to this day, as the great open door, the fresh possibility, the chance of a new start, for all who will confess the sin which is dragging them down, and will join in prayer for healing. When have you seen this "fresh possibility" launched with a confession of sins in community?

8. Forgiveness and healing are the two things which seem to push to the fore when we take our stand in the place where prayer makes sense, at the place where heaven and earth overlap, and at the place where our own present time and God's future time overlap.

   That is, after all, what Christian prayer, and for that matter Christian sacraments, are all about. Prayer isn't just me calling out in the dark to a distant or unknown God. It means what it means and does what it does because God is, as James promised, very near to those who draw near to him. Heaven and earth meet when, in the Spirit, someone calls on the name of the Lord. And it means what it means and does what it does because God's new time has broken into the continuing time of this sad old world, so that the person praying stands with one foot in the place of trouble, sickness and sin and with the other foot in the place of healing, forgiveness and hope. Prayer then brings the latter to bear on the former.

To understand all this may require some effort of the imagination. But once you've grasped it, prayer, like that puzzling musical instrument, can begin to play the tune it was designed to play. Suddenly it all makes sense.

In light of this, why do you think prayer is so terribly neglected in our culture?

9. In 1 Kings 17–18, the drought which came as judgment on the people of Israel, and the rain which came when they returned to the Lord and abandoned their idols, all happened in the context of Elijah's prayer. James emphasizes that prayer, of course, is not only a task for the "professionals," the clergy and Christian leaders. Every Christian has not only the right but the vocation to engage in prayer like that, prayer for one another, prayer for the sick, prayer for the sinners, prayer for the nation and the world. If everyone who reads these words were to determine to devote half an hour every day to this task, the effect could be incalculable.

Why is it tempting to think that Christian "professionals" are different than the rest of us when it comes to things like prayer?

10. In what ways would you like to grow as a person who prays power-fully?

11. How could your Christian community engage more in prayer?

12. As ever, James brings things right down to the practical level as he fin-ishes. To see someone wandering off in a dangerous direction and do nothing about it is a tragic dereliction of duty. It may be hard to turn them back—they may insist that they are right and we are wrong!—but the effort must be made. James knows it can be done. Perhaps James was even thinking of himself, as he and his family did not fol-low his brother Jesus during Jesus' three years of public ministry, only to be brought fully to the truth by his resurrected Lord.

What themes throughout this letter from James can be applied to this effort to bring someone back?

PRAY

Prayer must surround everything else that we do, whether we're sad or happy, suffering or cheerful. When prayer is done that is based on the fact that the Christian stands at the overlap-point of heaven and earth, of the present and the future, a bit of heaven arrives on earth; a bit of God's future becomes real in the present. New life and forgiveness are there in person. Reflect on what prayer is and that "when a righteous person prays, that prayer carries great power."

Consider spending one half-hour a day to pray this week for one another, for the sick, for sinners, for the nation and the world.

Talk to the Lord about your life of prayer.

NOTE ON JAMES 5:15

James seems, again like Jesus himself, to have seen a connection between sin and ill health. Jesus warned (in John 9) against making too close a link, but at other times, for instance in Mark 2:1-12, it seems that forgiveness and healing went hand in hand.

GUIDELINES FOR LEADERS

My grace is sufficient for you.
(2 Corinthians 12:9)

If leading a small group is something new for you, don't worry. These sessions are designed to flow naturally and be led easily. You may even find that the studies seem to lead themselves!

This study guide is flexible. You can use it with a variety of groups—students, professionals, coworkers, friends, neighborhood or church groups. Each study takes forty-five to sixty minutes in a group setting.

You don't need to be an expert on the Bible or a trained teacher to lead a small group. These guides are designed to facilitate a group's discussion, not a leader's presentation. Guiding group members to discover together what the Bible has to say and to listen together for God's guidance will help them remember much more than a lecture would.

There are some important facts to know about group dynamics and encouraging discussion. The suggestions listed below should equip you to effectively and enjoyably fulfill your role as leader.

PREPARING FOR THE STUDY

1. Ask God to help you understand and apply the passage in your own life. Unless this happens, you will not be prepared to lead others. Pray too for the various members of the group. Ask God to open your hearts to the message of his Word and motivate you to action.

2. Read the introduction to the entire guide to get an overview of the topics that will be explored.

3. As you begin each study, read and reread the assigned Bible passage to familiarize yourself with it. This study guide is based on the For Everyone series on the New Testament (published by SPCK and Westminster John Knox). It will help you and the group if you have on hand a copy of the companion volume from the For Everyone series both for the translation of the passage found there and for further insight into the passage.

4. Carefully work through each question in the study. Spend time in meditation and reflection as you consider how to respond.

5. Write your thoughts and responses in the space provided in the study guide. This will help you to express your understanding of the passage clearly.

6. It may help to have a Bible dictionary handy. Use it to look up any unfamiliar words, names or places. The glossary at the end of each New Testament for Everyone commentary may likewise be helpful for keeping discussion moving.

7. Reflect seriously on how you need to apply the Scripture to your life. Remember that the group members will follow your lead in responding to the studies. They will not go any deeper than you do.

LEADING THE STUDY

1. At the beginning of your first time together, explain that these studies are meant to be discussions, not lectures. Encourage the members of the group to participate. However, do not put pressure on those who may be hesitant to speak—especially during the first few sessions.

2. Be sure that everyone in your group has a study guide. Encourage the group to prepare beforehand for each discussion by reading the introduction to the guide and by working through the questions in each study.

3. Begin each study on time. Open with prayer, asking God to help the group to understand and apply the passage.

4. Have a group member read aloud the introduction at the beginning of the discussion.

5. Discuss the "Open" question before the Bible passage is read. The "Open" question introduces the theme of the study and helps group members to begin to open up, and can reveal where our thoughts and feelings need to be transformed by Scripture. Reading the passage first will tend to color the honest reactions people would otherwise give—because they are, of course, supposed to think the way the Bible does. Encourage as many members as possible to respond to the "Open" question, and be ready to get the discussion going with your own response.

6. Have a group member read aloud the passage to be studied as indicated in the guide.

7. The study questions are designed to be read aloud just as they are written. You may, however, prefer to express them in your own words.

   There may be times when it is appropriate to deviate from the study guide. For example, a question may have already been answered. If so, move on to the next question. Or someone may raise an important question not covered in the guide. Take time to discuss it, but try to keep the group from going off on tangents.

8. Avoid answering your own questions. An eager group quickly becomes passive and silent if members think the leader will do most of the talking. If necessary repeat or rephrase the question until it is clearly understood, or refer to the commentary woven into the guide to clarify the context or meaning.

9. Don't be afraid of silence in response to the discussion questions. People may need time to think about the question before formulating their answers.

10. Don't be content with just one answer. Ask, "What do the rest of you think?" or "Anything else?" until several people have given answers to the question.

11. Try to be affirming whenever possible. Affirm participation. Never reject an answer; if it is clearly off-base, ask, "Which verse led you to that conclusion?" or again, "What do the rest of you think?"

12. Don't expect every answer to be addressed to you, even though this will probably happen at first. As group members become more at ease, they will begin to truly interact with each other. This is one sign of healthy discussion.

13. Don't be afraid of controversy. It can be very stimulating. If you don't resolve an issue completely, don't be frustrated. Explain that the group will move on and God may enlighten all of you in later sessions.

14. Periodically summarize what the group has said about the passage. This helps to draw together the various ideas mentioned and gives continuity to the study. But don't preach.

15. Conclude your time together with the prayer suggestion at the end of the study, adapting it to your group's particular needs as appropriate. Ask for God's help in following through on the applications you've identified.

16. End on time.

Many more suggestions and helps for studying a passage or guiding discussion can be found in *How to Lead a LifeGuide Bible Study* and *The Big Book on Small Groups* (both from InterVarsity Press/USA).

Other InterVarsity Press Resources from N. T. Wright

The Challenge of Jesus
N. T. Wright offers clarity and a full accounting of the facts of the life and teachings of Jesus, revealing how the Son of God was also solidly planted in first-century Palestine. *978-0-8308-2200-3, 202 pages, hardcover*

The Challenge of Easter
The meaning of Easter seems lost among the colored eggs and chocolate candies. In this excerpt from *The Challenge of Jesus*, N. T. Wright explains Easter's bold, almost unbelievable claim: Jesus has risen from the dead. Here is God's announcement of an invitation to live as though God is among us, making everything new. *978-0-8308-3848-6, 64 pages, paperback*

Resurrection
This 50-minute DVD confronts the most startling claim of Christianity—that Jesus rose from the dead. Shot on location in Israel, Greece and England, N. T. Wright presents the political, historical and theological issues of Jesus' day and today regarding this claim. Wright brings clarity and insight to one of the most profound mysteries in human history. Study guide included. *978-0-8308-3435-8, DVD*

Evil and the Justice of God
N. T. Wright explores all aspects of evil and how it presents itself in society today. Fully grounded in the story of the Old and New Testaments, this presentation is provocative and hopeful; a fascinating analysis of and response to the fundamental question of evil and justice that faces believers. *978-0-8308-3398-6, 176 pages, hardcover*

Evil
Filmed in Israel, South Africa and England, this 50-minute DVD confronts some of the major "evil" issues of our time—from tsunamis to AIDS—and puts them under the biblical spotlight. N. T. Wright says there is a solution to the problem of evil, if only we have the honesty and courage to name it and understand it for what it is. Study guide included. *978-0-8308-3434-1, DVD*

Small Faith—Great God
N. T. Wright reminds us that what matters is not how much faith we have but Who our faith is in. Wright looks at the character of the faith God calls us to. He unfolds how dependence, humility and mystery all have a role to play. But the author doesn't ignore the messiness and difficulties of life, when hard times come and the unexpected knocks us down. He opens to us what faith means in times of trial and even in the face of death. Through it all he reminds us, it's not great faith we need: it is faith in a great God. *978-0-8308-3833-2, 176 pages, hardcover*

Justification: God's Plan and Paul's Vision
In this comprehensive account and defense of the crucial doctrine of justification, Wright also responds to critics who have challenged what has come to be called the New Perspective. Ultimately, he provides a chance for those in the middle of and on both sides of the debate to interact directly with his views and form their own conclusions. *978-0-8308-3863-9, 279 pages, hardcover*

Colossians and Philemon
In Colossians, Paul presents Christ as "the firstborn over all creation," and appeals to his readers to seek a maturity found only in Christ. In Philemon, Paul appeals to a fellow believer to receive a runaway slave in love and forgiveness. In this volume N. T. Wright offers comment on both of these important books. *978-0-8308-4242-1, 199 pages, paperback*